Owl at Twilight

TO KATE,
ALL THE BEST,
MATT XX

Mario Relich, who grew up in Montreal, holds dual citizenship, Canadian and British, and lives in Edinburgh. His MA in English Literature is from McGill University, and his PhD, on the same subject, from the University of Edinburgh. He has been an Associate Lecturer in English Literature and Film History at the Open University in Scotland, and Post-Colonial Literature for the London Open University Literature MA programme. He has also taught Film Studies at the Edinburgh College of Art. For nearly twenty years, he was Programme Secretary of the Poetry Association of Scotland. Over the years, he has published poems, both in hard-copy and online periodicals, in Scotland, Canada, and England. *Owl at Twilight* is his second collection of poetry.

Owl at Twilight

Mario Relich

Kennedy & Boyd
an imprint of
Zeticula Ltd
Unit 13
196 Rose Street,
Edinburgh,
EH2 4AT,
Scotland.

http://www.kennedyandboyd.co.uk
admin@kennedyandboyd.co.uk

First published in 2021
Copyright © Mario Relich 2021

Cover Image Copyright © Dennis Buchner 2021
Photo by Dennis Buchner on Unsplash.com

ISBN 978-1-84921-224-3

To Wanda

Acknowledgements

All the poems were written during the past seven years, after my first collection *Frisky Ducks* (Grace Note Publications, 2014). Some of the poems have appeared in *Southlight*, *The (Glasgow) Herald*, in Lesley Duncan's column 'Poem of the Day', and *Scottish Affairs*, edited by Michael Rosie. My poems have also appeared in the online journals *Gitanjali and Beyond* and Richie McCaffery's *The Lyrical Aye*. I read a number of the poems for *The Heretics*, at the Waverley Bar in Edinburgh, and a few times for the 'Poetry and Coffee' sessions at Henderson's Restaurant, at the invitation of Henry Marsh, and also the Poetry Association of Scotland, hosted by the Scottish Poetry Library. My poem 'Indiana Jones' appeared in *A Kyst of Thistles: An anthology of radical poetry from contemporary Scotland*, edited by Jim Aitken, and published by *Culture Matters*.

I would particularly like to thank Vicki Feaver, Elspeth Brown, and Kate Hendry, as well as William Hershaw, Stewart Conn, and Gordon Wright. All provided valuable advice, and stimulating discussion, on the art and craft of poetry. Their views on poetry and poets are of immense value to me. My own poems, of course, are solely my responsibility.

Among supportive friends whose encouragement was most welcome, I would like to mention Tom Hubbard, Ian Wood, Bashabi Fraser, Joy Hendry, Joyce Caplan, Roy Dalgleish, Liz Szewczyk, John Lodge, and Frank Birbalsingh. Family connections I have always found sustaining in my writing, first and foremost, my wife Wanda, my step-daughter Bridget, my step-son David; and in Sydney, my brother Joe, my sister-in-law Jo-Anne, and my nephews Joe, Jr and Javier, and my niece Jinnez.

Contents

Prologue

*'There are two ways of spreading light: to be the candle or
the mirror that reflects it.'*
Edith Wharton, The Age of Innocence

Honoured Shade: Robert Garioch

Honoured Shade: Robert Garioch

It was an era when most of the poets
I knew were men, that's just how it was
in Scotland. The first one I remember
was Robert Garioch, so friendly to me,

a stranger from Montreal, Canada.
He invited me to contribute poems
to *Scottish International*. His classes
on Scottish writers, which he taught

at the University of Edinburgh,
opened up new vistas for me, his own
poems in Scots a revelation, modern,
not archaic. The Enlightenment for him

wasn't that long ago, which is why
he objected to the naming of the David
Hume Tower in 'A Wee Local Scandal'.
Scunnered, in that poem he suggested

that it should have been named
'The Will Cleghorn Erection',
since the university hypocritically
honoured a mediocre nonentity,

over Hume, with a professorship.
But 'the whirligig of time brings in
his revenges.' 'Cancelled', his name
no longer adorns the 'wee skyscraper'.

His obscure footnote about Africans,
is deemed offensive today, yet he argued
against slavery and the slave trade.
No matter, zealots still hate David Hume.

Like Hume, Garioch was a moderate,
and he would have hated today's
self-righteous trolls, who reject any kind
of civilized debate with anyone.

Garioch, we have urgent need of you
at this hour, so very good in casting
a sharp eye on the city's 'high heid yins',
but always siding with sceptical citizens.

I

Canal Scenes

'It's not what you look at that matters, it's what you see.'
Henry David Thoreau

Along the Canal

While I walked along the canal,
a female goosander swam closely,
right beside me, her crested head
and proud beak held up so high
and elegantly that the mallards
quacking nearby couldn't compete,
dignity of any kind not their style,
cousins perhaps, but too common.

A cormorant, grooming itself,
its wings outstretched, solitary,
stood like the Angel of the North,
on the canal bank, stolidly silent.

Walking alone at my own brisk pace,
the minutes stilled to a state of grace.

Banana Boat

On the other side of the canal,
hedged by trees and bushes, I saw
a rowboat intensely yellow
like a newly ripened banana.

Bobbing gently up and down,
its stern curved, like its prow:
it seemed totally abandoned,
rippling with its mirror-image.

That shimmer of restless yellow
conjured up sunlit memories
of a banana-shaped coffin
parading through a village.

A rich fruit-merchant in Ghana
commissioned such a sendoff,
easily dismissed as ostentatious,
but really a tribute to his life.

Goosanders on a Wintry Day

I love goosanders, with their sharp, curved beaks,
more stately than the other ducks I saw on the canal.
One was a male, its head green-glossed black,
and beside it was a chestnut-crested female.

The male dived carefree, the female hardly stirred,
while the sun shone brightly on a crisp, cold day.
The goosander diving under seemed completely lost,
leaving only a placid ripple, resurfacing elsewhere

like fugitive thoughts reminding me they never
really die, thoughts that return as if what we forget
is never completely lost, they hide in the depths
like decoys. The goosanders distracted me

from dark thoughts which cast a shadow
when I was in too self-absorbed a state,
their majestic calm such a welcome respite,
so that even nosey mallards steered clear.

Nuthatch

(To Vicki Feaver)

Noticing the undergrowth of a wooded area,
I could hear the sound of the bird's persistent
'wheet, wheet, wheet'. Its camouflage blue-gray,
and rusty, the nuthatch foraged among twigs:

It looked like barely a whirr, as it it flew up
to a branch. Its streak of black through the eyes,
made him a highwayman; not really frightening,
but insects on the ground had to scatter.

Magpie Poems

I

Hidden Magpie

Something stirred in the undergrowth
of a cotoneaster shrub, which startled me.
It was a magpie, silently feasting on berries.
My unwelcome presence made it fly out
in a hurry, its chatter like the 'rat-tat-tat'
of a relentless machine-gun stutter.

It stretched out its wings in gliding motion.
During the late Jurassic period, its ancestor
the archaeopterix might have glided
in a similar way, swooping mercilessly
on our own predecessors, puny rodent-like
mammals slinking away from sky terror.

Magpie beaks have a sharp cutting-edge,
very useful as they have no compunction
raiding other birds' nests, devouring their eggs,
and sometimes their young. Inhuman, isn't it?
Do not be let the purplish-blue iridescence
of their dinosaur-inherited wings fool you.

II

Magpies Overhead

A couple of chattering magpies perched
    on swaying bare branches
of a slender tree, their alarm answered by a
    solitary one balanced
on an electricity pole across the other side of the canal.

It was a dead magpie sprawled with bluish-purple
    wings outstretched,
walkers side-stepping it, some very carefully,
    possibly disturbed
by what it meant, which caused the commotion
    that blustery day.

Before long, a crowd of magpies appeared
    from the overcast sky,
like a sudden fleet of warplanes,
    their cacophony of wailing cries
aggravated by the cat, its jaws blood-wet,
    hiding in the bushes.

Sparrows at Large

I

Autumn Sparrows

Bramble bushes beside me,
sparrows hidden there:
they navigate from thorn
to thorn, like tropical fish
in coral reefs, darting away
if you stare at them too hard,
or so I briefly imagine.

These sparrows' camouflage
is not so colourful as coral;
the bushes, like them, brownish,
while they hide from passers-by.
Revealed by boisterous twittering,
cheerful, or alarmed, out of sight,
above all, they are brashly present.

II

Foraging Sparrows

When I saw sparrows,
shrill, very energetic,
on the bare branches
of a small ash tree,

sunshine intensely bright
on a frosty winter morning,
I liked to hear how happy
they seemed to sound.

And yet all they wanted
was to find a better place,
the grass beneath too frozen,
and look for stray insects,

or even bread-crumbs,
quizzical at each other,
desperately hungry,
while complaining loudly.

Pied Wagtail

A lone wagtail looks marooned,
on a piece of ice; it's a cold day,
but sunshine melts icy fragments
floating lazily on the canal.

Nearby a purposeful swan
approaches like a Viking ship
intent on scattering the ice-floe,
and yet it glides so quietly.

Out of the depths, a female
goosander, its crest displayed,
suddenly emerges, as it splashes
noisily before flying skyward.

It's early spring, but the wagtail
back from abroad, so starkly pied,
black and white, unmistakeable,
simply finds it too unseasonal.

Too cold, it twitches its tail
on its sheet of moving ice,
and it's a sure bet that it won't
find any insects, not this time.

Suburban Winter Birds

A couple of bullfinches called to each other;
their sharp, restless chirping while darting
from branch to branch among red berries,
one at the end the rowan tree's top branch,
the other lower down on the canal bank.
It was a cold, dreich day, but their black heads,
orange chests, and bluish grey wings,
brightened it with a blaze of colour.

Nearby, on an exposed bit of ground, a kind
of suburban *no man's land,* a blackbird
foraged among the dead leaves still left
from autumn. As soon as it saw me coming,
it flew to the roof of a small conservatory
across the fence in a neighbour's garden.
No doubt for the blackbird I disturbed,
property was not theft, but a safe haven.

Walking to another small, public area,
which was a bower made up of scraggly,
bare-branched trees, I saw a robin hiding
in a thorny thistle bush, but it broke cover
and flew to the top of a tree. It didn't
much feel like chirping, and just perched
very still on a thin branch, hoping perhaps
that I would get out soon, and leave it be.

II

Personal Poems

'The personal is always personal.'

Banquo

The Invisible Enemy

The Portable Voltaire

Moriarty

Freya's Cat

Winter Solstice

Venetian Memory

Chaffinch

Banquo

(i.m. Eberhard 'Paddy' Bort)

It's a pub I liked to frequent,
and have a drink with friends,
conversing about anything
which took our fancy,
politics and art foremost.

And you, you liked to talk
about the crime novel:
Rankin, yes, but Simenon
much better; you read him
in English and in German.

The Oak near Old College
was friendly to all folkies
who strummed their guitars,
and sang ballads, whether
any good at it or not.

If they sang too loudly
you frowned at them,
telling them what's what:
we looked at each other,
smiling, shrugging it off.

But a sudden heart-attack
ambushed you late at night
and your life brutally ended,
I can't go back there now:
your ghost would haunt me.

The Invisible Enemy

A blackbird came out of the undergrowth
and flew to the nearest hedge, as I entered
a fenced-in area of barren, leafless trees.
Distracted, I almost missed a blue tit
flying low, a miniature Spitfire compared
to the bulkier Hurricane of the blackbird
which had disappeared. Looking back
at another anxious time, we are so lucky
that dive-bombers aren't deliberately
spraying us with machine-gun fire.

Yet, we can't be complacent, for we are
in no way out of harm's way. The enemy
won't swoop down from the horizon,
but now it is invisible, and ready to strike
if we're careless, or our luck runs out.

The blackbirds, and blue tits you might see
in your garden, or wild areas, can cope
with predators. The greatest threat they face
comes only from ourselves, and so does
the invisibly ubiquitous, mutating foe.

The Portable Voltaire

I still have *The Portable Voltaire,* a book
my mother gave me for my birthday,
when I turned thirteen. Did she know
I was already something of an atheist; or,
in spite of her being a church-goer, was it
because she found a dog-eared paperback
of the free-thinking *Candide* in my room?

A gifted linguist herself, she tutored me
to prepare for an imminent exam in French.
We faced each other at the kitchen table,
both a bit bored, and practiced speaking it,
but the lesson ended with her singing softly
to herself 'Sous Les Ponts de Paris', her bridge
to the place where she really wanted to be.

Moriarty

I haven't seen you for a long time;
we really we have nothing in common.
It's possibly a matter of wariness
because we compete in what we do,
and sometimes get in each other's way,
even though totally separate in our orbits.

But Sherlock Holmes provides a clue
to our mutual hostility if we happen
to meet by chance, like the sleuth's
encounters with the ruthless Moriarty
in stories which test his ingenuity,
or luck, as in the Reichenbach Falls.

Moriarty was the epitome of evil,
indeed 'the Napoleon of crime', yet,
that wasn't why Holmes disliked him;
he was his dark shadow, his Mr Hyde.
You're Moriarty, I am Holmes, or
the other way round, it doesn't matter.

Freya's Cat

The Persian cat, larger
than most in this area,
saw me coming, and it froze.

He looked at me annoyed,
and it was so visibly *there*
in its bedraggled white fur.

We faced each other
at a distance, before
he crept underneath

his new owner's car,
a lucky cat, free to roam
the streets, his domain.

Until recently, he belonged
to Freya, a sweet-natured
and lively widow. No longer

could she care for him,
needing care herself.
For so long she wandered

aimlessly, waving 'Hi'
to everyone walking
near her bungalow,

but leaving her door open,
even in the worst weather,
until at last her family,

and district nurses,
saw her dementia was
too far advanced.

She left her old life
forever, a care home
nearby her destination.

Recently, we heard,
she packed her clothes
to frantically run away

she knew not where,
but her daimon, the cat,
still patrols our streets.

Winter Solstice

I could see nothing,
it was so totally dark,
I could have been blind,
a nightnare. I felt a fog

gradually enveloping me,
as I paced the deck
of an ocean liner, alone
and utterly frozen.

I caught a glimpse
of the shore, faint lights
blinking in the distance,
and the ship getting nearer.

What I desperately needed,
as I woke up, my blanket cold,
was the welcoming safety
of a landfall in the morning.

But as luck would have it,
I was dealt an ace of spades,
for I fell asleep again,
and this was my dream:

I stood on the deck,
and felt a shaft of pain,
ambushed by a shadow,
looming like an iceberg.

Venetian Memory

(in memory of Catherine Burns Relich, 1937-1983)

They tell you that the person you loved,
though she is now departed, will always
live on in your memory, so that should really
mitigate your sorrow: it's a consolation
devoutly to be wished. Well, no, it's not.

I see a square-shaped colour photograph
before me, and it's one of the woman
I loved, standing to the left, her face
slightly inclined to the right, and looking
at me, smiling, the sun caressing her.

She is in front of a bazaar displaying
delicate fabrics shimmering and colourful,
so summery in her rainbow-hued dress.
Her golden hair is seductively half-length,
and there is dramatic scene behind her.

It's a textile image of the Three Wise Men
bringing gifts to the Virgin Mary's child.
The moment barely lasted, but it's there
in the photograph, at least while I write,
and stored in the attic of my memory.

Yes, a visit to Venice in the high-summer
does yield memories to be treasured,
and we did feel very happy. I can't forget
having espresso coffee at St. Mark's Square.
Looking back, I ask myself, is that all there is?

Chaffinch

(*East Princes Street Gardens, Edinburgh*)

There it was, warbling vigorously,
no doubt staking out its territory.

I stopped, walking along a path
leading to the National Gallery,

and stood still, like a hunter,
listening closely with intent.

It was almost right beside me;
the path was on a gradient,

and the bird on a slightly swaying
slender branch of the leafy ash-tree

beside the path below, which is why
I could see the chaffinch so clearly,

at first mistaking it for a robin,
since its chest was red. Its head

was greyish-blue, and its wing
revealed a streak of white.

I recognised a colourful finch,
not rare, deemed rather common,

but my discovery was beyond
that of a mere ornithologist.

Freed from thinking for a while
or being too purposeful, the moment

was so sky-blue transporting,
that it seemed like infinity,

not like 'a galaxy far away' perhaps,
but a couple of minutes or so,

of unexpected, limitless pleasure,
and a sense of pure freedom,

it can never be denied,
that comes, when it comes.

III

Art and Artists

*'All art is a memory of age-old things, dark things, whose
fragments live on in the artist.'*
Paul Klee

The Black Archer

An American Visitor at Abbotsford

Wellington

James Tissot: Chrysanthemums

Skulls

February Sun

Apples

Homage to William Gear

The Black Archer

Painted on oak panel, circa 1640,
and now in the Wallace Collection,
the half-length portrait, called a *tronie*
in Dutch, of an African boy, is darkly lit
and colour-coded, mainly in shades
of gold and black. He was identified
for a long time as Rembrandt's model,
and was certainly painted in his studio,
probably by Govert Flinck, reputedly
the Old Master's favourite pupil.

The pensive boy's hunting-jacket
looks like dark-brown leather,
but with a golden sheen. He firmly
grasps a bow in his right hand,
an elegant lace cravat at his neck,
and a quiver of arrows over his shoulder,
not a page-boy, but a young aristocrat.
The real story behind the portrait,
and what kind of life the boy had lived,
is lost, perhaps in an obscure archive.

Was he an Amsterdam merchant's
family servant, or was he 'loaned'
to the studio by the city orphanage?
How well did Rembrandt treat him?
Was he a friend of Flinck's, one
who found freedom, however tenuous,
in the studio? But immortality of a kind
he did achieve. Whether Rembrandt
painted him or not, his mystery remains:
a past life haunting us with ambiguities.

An American Visitor at Abbotsford

When Sir Walter Scott met John James Audubon
his guest in Abbotsford, he marvelled at the American's
ornithological accuracy, evident in the way he drew
so many kinds of birds in the New World. He brought
to our eyes the magnificent splendour of their plumage,
and strategies for camouflage, their habitats the forests,
mountains and plains of a continent still barely explored.
It was quite unknown territory to Scott — himself
nicknamed 'The Great Unknown' — but immense.
America seemed wild and untamed, like the Highlands
and Islands in Scotland's folk memory after Culloden.

Despite Audubon's French roots, Scott remarked
in his *Journal* that *he was less of a Frenchman
than I have ever seen – no dash, or glimmer, or shine
about him.* Similarly, he acknowledged that although
his drawings accurately depicted every species of bird
he found in his explorations, such as a flamingo so tall,
he had to draw its pink neck and partly reddish beak
bending down to the bottom corner of the colour-plate,
itself life-sized, or a bald eagle tearing at the belly
of a dead, upturned catfish. The *animated depiction*
of a snake attacking a bird's nest, appealed to Scott's
sense of drama, yet he also recorded his reservation
that such *extreme correctness rather gives a stiffness
to the drawings.* He thought that they lacked any sense,
so it seems, of soaring, unrestricted, palpitating life,
his visitor *having no knowledge of* **virtu,** his patrician
word for a spark of artistic and decidedly manly vitality.

Wellington

Ignore the biographers, all intent,
on his military and political exploits,
his family relationships, and no doubt
a dalliance or two. It's better to study
his portraits. If you visit Apsley House,
called No. 1, London, in his honour,
there you'll find Thomas Lawrence's
painting of Wellington in his prime,
a black sash across his Field Marshal's
red jacket, campaign medal like a star,
only a few months before Waterloo.

His arms are folded and he looks you
in the eye, as if he'd told the painter,
Be quick about it man, you know
I haven't got all day; even less time
than he might have thought: Napoleon,
exiled in Elba, was plotting his escape.

A starker portrait, at the National Gallery,
and one of Goya's finest, done in Spain
at the sombre climax of Wellington's
Peninsular Campaign, reveals his face
unshaven and more care-worn, his red jacket
looking slightly faded, less resplendent,
but more bestrewn with medals,
the cruciform badge of the Spanish
Order of the Golden Fleece hanging
by a long, elaborate ribbon from his neck.

He looks past us, barely bothering to pose,
pre-occupied, it seems, with what destiny
holds for him, and he could just as easily
tear off his decorations, not quite a hero
to himself, or the artist, but just a man.

By 1844, a daguerrotype by Antoine Claudet,
stored where he lived last, Stratfield Saye House,
shows Wellington at his most relaxed,
white-haired, sporting a loose-fitting
dark jacket and buttoned-up white shirt.

For the first time, light silvered in copper
captured the former military hero, who was
rather less popular as former Tory PM,
at heart Anglo-Irish and aristocratic,
yet who also insisted on and brought about
Catholic emancipation. In this photograph
the 'Iron Duke' just looks like a kindly
Victorian grandfather: straight in his bearing,
yet so ghostly he could almost vanish.

Skulls

A friar, heavily cowled, his face so shadowed
as to be barely visible, kneels and looks up.
He holds a skull whose eye-sockets stare at him
as he prays fervently, seeking a God elusive
and invisible, the brushstrokes just black and brown.
Behold Zurbaran's austerely magnificent
Spanish painting, *St Francis in Meditation.*

Cezanne's *Still Life with Skull,* is sombre, less devoted,
and pictorially strangely exotic in his treatment
of ordinary fruit. The dark yellowed skull on the table
has socketless eyes, oblivious to the luscious fruit
carefully arranged on the table: apples, pears, one lemon,
and one peach freshly picked, its green leaf still attached.
sensuality predominant in the entire composition.

But an isolated pear surrounded by a folded, pure white
linen tablecloth, as if protected from the skull, reminds us
that for Cezanne 'death is the fruit of life.' His title,
nature morte au crane, has a precise French elegance,
which suits such an eloquent transformation of still life.

When Basquiat tried his hand at his version of
            memento mori,
it was a matter of compulsion, his life was so precarious,
Boom for Real his catchphrase. He could hardly have dreamed
his painting, **Untitled**, so enigmatic about death, would sell
for a record breaking price at an art auction in New York.
his home town, long after his life was cut short, overdosed
on drugs, when he was still only 27.

He portrays the face of a man, his expression fiercely rigid,
whose skull shows through in rainbow colours, outlined
by heavy black lines, the canvas mostly blue. The painting
pulsates between life and death, so gritty and much
      like graffiti,
that it throbs with violent defiance, that of an artist
      subliminally,
if not sublimely American.

James Tissot: Chrysanthemums

That's his wife toiling in their garden,
just taken by surprise, but looking graceful
wearing a bonnet and yellow shawl.
Crouching down, her left hand
outstretched, and holding the stem
of a white chrysanthemum in her right one,
she looks at him with mocking displeasure,
possibly asking: 'Do you call that work?'

Blooms appear ready for plucking
above her: the painting's top half
is crowded with them, a symphony
of lemon yellow, pale gold,
vibrant orange, and lilac varieties
of chrysanthemums shining
with strong blazing colours:
flowers shimmering in sunlight.

Perhaps James Tissot had seen
the crouching marble Venus
when visiting the British Museum,
severely Hellenistic in hairstyle,
and herself imperiously naked,
delicately hiding her breasts
with a contemptuous look,
as if surprised in her bath.

The goddess he so admired,
looked classically voluptuous,
even if coldly enigmatic,
but the earth-bound portrait
of his wife tending their garden,
does have its own appeal:
the artist transformed her
into a modern Persephone.

February Sun

Outside, it's pure ice, my eyes briefly blinded
by the sun: I look instead at the pale sky
blue as the elegant Tiepolo would have painted it
but the stationary clouds more like Constable's.

Yet Tiepolo's sky was a warm, Italian one,
and Constable's clouds, usually summery,
but this is Scotland in winter, bracing and cold,
even as the sun's rays hint at an early Spring.

Once, long ago, shaggy mammoths
Roamed in a snowy landscape only Breughel
could have painted. Distant hunters,
Neanderthals, looked up at the sun.

Apples

Let's start by looking at Van Gogh's
'Still Life With Apples'. The background
looks earthy, with greenish-brownish
splashes of colour. The apples translucent,
and restlessly red, yet their texture seems
like that of large onions, as if Van Gogh
suggests how enticingly nutritious they are
for hungry workmen, since nothing here
reminds us of a bourgeois kitchen,
the background not even a tablecloth.

Cezanne's 'Still Life With Apples and a Tube
of Paint' gives us a close-up of his apples,
seven in all, tightly linked together.
The splashy green background is light
and soothing, inviting us to contemplate
a rich array of the fruit in varying shades
of red, and one much closer to yellow.
Greenish shadows are discreetly present, while
we catch a glimpse of the white tube of paint,
Cezanne mocking nostalgia for 'trompe l'oil'.

Lucian Freud was just seventeen in 1939
when he painted 'Box of Apples in Wales',
his own roughing up of 'still life' conventions:
it's just a wooden crate full of orchard apples
jumbled together ready to be marketed,
and a couple of them arbitrarily overspilled.
Dark brown ridge lines of the mountain backdrop
create a stark wilderness in which the artist
could paint them with such concentration
that these apples look intoxicatingly real.

But in 'The Listening Room', Magritte, more mature,
played a bolder game. An entire room is taken up
by his enigmatic apple, like an estate agent's nightmare,
a dark shadow to its right, and reflected sunlight
from a window, in which sea and sky are visible,
on the other. Too huge to constitute a 'still life'
by a Dutch Old Master , it is yet paradoxically close
to the visual accuracy of such paintings. The apple,
bright green, is almost perfectly spherical,
revealing Magritte's sense of a hidden alchemy.

Homage to William Gear

There is no right or wrong to it, it's only what sticks in your brain.
Gallery attendant at City Art Centre, Edinburgh

Spring Landscape

What hits us right between the eyes
is an explosion of blinding colours,
sharp like shrapnel, black shapes
floating downwards, making way
in a narrow, vertical canvas,
to nearly pointillistic daubs
of pinks, yellows, and greens.

Red Summer

It's such a luminous shimmer:
jagged red shards looking faintly
like pterodactyls, their large,
membrane-like wings overhead.
They glide upwards only to disappear
like an optical illusion, but the sun
is still felt with Turneresque energy.

Autumn Landscape

Some lozenge-like, swirling,
shifting shapes of yellow, red,
and white, the background
embedded in ochre. Lineaments
of a face-mask just discernible,
decompose the leafy scatterings
in biomorphic, web-like lines.

November Landscape

The deepening dark heralds
approaching winter days,
or memories of war. Shafts
of loose black, linear shapes
drizzle like rain falling aslant;
brushstrokes smudge the canvas,
like flowers in trench mud.

Winter Landscape

Geometric in its elaborations,
it's a canvas which overwhelms
with its march of black verticals
and splashes of reds and yellows.
Yet there's still something
like a shadow, which appears
to darken the snow.

March Landscape

A vertical, grid-like pattern
of layered, crooked lines
like seams of Fife coal
which the artist's father,
had mined, the background
beige, white and grey, but also
with flecks of sunny yellow.

Sussex Landscape

It's so much like an aerial view,
the artist at his most freewheeling.
If a plane flew really high,
like a spacecraft, the view would
be very much his abstract vision:
a mesh of thick lines, and black coils
among blazing colours.

IV

Places

Carlsbad Caverns

I've never been there, yet in my mind's eye I can
see Carlsbad Caverns, their location a secret to me
as a child, but actually in the Guadalupe Mountains
of New Mexico, an area thronged with tourists now,
and a designated National Park since Calvin Coolidge.
With fearsome names like Bottomless Pit, the caves
haunt my memory, as I recall their effect on me,
which was not quite sinister, but unfathomable.

And I remember how thrilled I was at the age of 12
to focus my eyes on my primitive plastic View- Master
stereoscope, clicking one 3-D double-slide after another
of The Big Room, a limestone chamber, as gigantic
as any cathedral interior, with its columnar array
of stalactites like huge icicles brightening the dark.

Dunbar

(to Elspeth Brown)

Walking along the street
near the seashore, I saw
a derelict house, its garden
full of rampant weeds.

It rained hard, and the house
looked like a ruin 'knocked about
a bit' when Dunbar felt the full force
of Cromwell's saturnine temper.

Among the weeds, a blaze
of bright red poppies
Nolde could have painted,
lightened the overcast gloom.

Dieppe

Just across the English Channel,
Dieppe has seen better days;
its luck changed since the Allied
raid in August 1942 destroyed
its famous Casino. In the past,
it brought no luck to Oscar Wilde,
in exile after leaving Reading Gaol,
De Profundis his testament,
and hounded by the better class
of tourists visiting from London.

Walter Sickert, an old friend
who lived in Dieppe, avoided him
even at the Café des Tribunaux,
which visitors still frequent.
He painted its murky, dimly-lit
façade, depicting, in purple
and magenta, street-lighting
against the night, colours Wilde
would have appreciated
for their boldly garish quality.

Sickert also painted *The Façade*
Of St. Jacques. Wilde most likely
visited the High Gothic church
to contemplate his disastrous
fall from grace, and the prospect
of a futile future. Like Melmoth,
his alter-ego in France, he became
a wanderer, following his nemesis,
and ertswhile lover, Lord Alfred Douglas,
absent at his death in a Paris hotel.

A few years later, J. D. Fergusson,
the Scottish Colourist, painted *Dieppe,*
14 July 1905, a chromatic exploration
of the fireworks across the harbour,
which celebrated Bastille Day.
A throng of the fashionably-dressed
at the bottom third of the canvas,
lit up in their nocturnal promenade.
Tonally, it's a feast of exuberant, reds,
whites, and blues: Dieppe in its heyday.

Glasgow Central Station

I watched her on the platform,
looking attractive and self-assured,
a purely idle moment, I admit.

Out of the corner of my eye,
I saw a famous writer, running
for his train, just catching it.

He had re-imagined Glasgow,
and he was, I could see, on his way
to Edinburgh, his capital city.

By the time I left for the exit,
a motorcyclist revved up,
tooting at lassies in the steet.

I felt watched by the statue
of squat Citizen Firefighter,
inscrutable in oxygen mask.

Looking Across

(for my niece, Jinnez)

Across the Embankment, in front of us
the dome of Saint Paul's, the Shard
behind us, we sat on a bench, both
looking at the night sky, each
preoccupied with drifting thoughts.

To our left, the sun was a bright orange slowly
sinking down, and its rays still lighting up the sky,
yet to our right it was totally dark, the stars shining
towards the East End, the River Thames murky.

We sat and talked in desultory manner
about how unusual we found this to be.
It could have been an eclipse of the sun,
but for revellers cruising back and forth.

The Temple Church, London

The Temple Church along King's Bench Walk
between Fleet Street and the River Thames,
provides a portal to the Templars in their prime:
left of the entrance lie their helmeted effigies.

If you look carefully, the knights recumbent,
are splendidly awake, clutching their swords
and stony shields, their staring eyes wide open,
chivalrous, ready to face the Last Judgement.

In life, they fought for Jerusalem, sacred to them,
and as Christians theirs by right, or so they decreed.
If the church itself suffered damage during the Blitz,
the Election after VE Day promised a New Jerusalem.

The Templars will still be here for a thousand years,
but chances are just as ruins. Pilgrim tourists
may always treasure this hallowed space, seeking
another entry to their own imagined Jerusalem.

Oslo

My portal to Oslo, purely on a whim,
starts with Ibsen: I like the bronze statue
of Ibsen as a forbidding, frock-coated
gentleman standing tall, his face covered
in abundant bushy sideburns, and long hair
brushed back from his ample forehead.
His piercing look almost orders you
to enter the National Theatre of Norway,
its portico like that of an Athenian temple,
perhaps to see *A Doll's House* or *Hedda Gabler*,
and learn lessons about how to achieve
freedom from the stiflingly conventional.

Next stop is the Vigeland Sculpture Park, entered
by its own Gates of Paradise. Gustav Vigeland's
exuberant figurative sculptures, bronze, or stone,
hyper-activity the keynote, greet us everywhere
in the rampant nakedness of men, women,
children and family groups, energetically athletic
in their poses, and happiness predominant.
It's a festival of innocence, like Adam and Eve's,
yet even here the Fall intrudes, embodied
in the confrontational 'Angry Boy'. Larger than life,
a bronze little giant, he looks decidedly unhappy,
yet reputed to be the most popular with visitors.

More intimately, an online book festival I recall
had Linn Ullmann, daughter of Ingmar Bergman
and Liv Ullmann, her study in a well-appointed
Oslo flat, talking about her novel-memoir *Unquiet*.
Since Bergman and Ullmann were married,
'but not to each other', her birth was unwelcome,
but she shrugged it off as 'I was a scandal'.
She observed that 'families are tiny societies,
and that is why a seemingly innocuous comment,
like *pass the pepper, darling* at a dinner-party
can turn out to be lethal.' Golden sunlight
enhanced her face like a Bergman close-up.

Global Shades of Pink

Looking at the Amazon river dolphins,
friendly to the fishermen in their boats,
they remind us of other dolphins
we might see in open-air aquariums
or television wild-life documentaries,

ducking, diving, and jumping up high,
even if not pursuing any fish, nor reward.
But nothing, unless you know the river,
can prepare us for dolphins displaying
themselves in the fleeting shimmer

of startling pink flashes beckoning
us to follow them deliriously,
looking for a good time, and careless
of the amphibious black caiman,
a sinister, gloomy croc hidden below.

Another living, breathing creature
bright as the dolphins, if more lethargic
is the pink iguana, and it's to be found
totally isolated in the Galapagos,
living on the luxuriant, shiny green

vegetation growing on the slopes
of the smouldering Wolf volcano
in the lush island of Isabela,
Darwin, had he known about them,
like the other iguanas he saw there,

would have wondered how
such a freakish reptile happened
to evolve its pinkish coloration,
so far from 'red in tooth and claw',
and observed that its sensitive skin

allows the blood in its veins
to look pink on the outside.
A creature far too proximate
to an active volcano, it's rare
and found nowhere else.

Less endangered, but elusive,
the pink robin can be found
in the remote rainforests
of southeastern Australia.
Small and sooty-feathered,

apart from its lilac pink chest,
it's quietly unobtrusive, and
often looks for insects, but it's not
related to the robins I sometimes see
in my back-garden, just as diligent:

pearly in pink, it pleases the eye
like the red of robins in winter;
river, volcano, and rainforest, all
are habitats in which animals
pink in pigment still survive,
quirks of opulent evolution.

V

Writers

'Odd how the creative power at once brings the whole universe to order.'
Virginia Woolf

Robert Fergusson in the Canongate

to Tom Hubbard

Fergusson in front of the Canongate Kirk
looks as if he's just risen from his grave
in the old kirkyard behind him, brought
to life for a brisk walk in the Royal Mile.

'Very small and delicate,' he looked
to some, 'a little in-kneed, and
vaiguing in his walk,' but his eyes
could pierce you, it was said.

The poet may have met David Hume
and Adam Smith in oyster taverns,
perhaps even in Luckie Middlemist's,
the Cowgate howff in *Caller Oysters.*

He liked his oysters and rich ale,
warding off his fear of damnation
by incipient madness, all too prescient
when hallucinations gripped his mind.

Wearing a straw crown, he was left
to die in the bedlam of Darien House,
but David Annand's jaunty statue
does not even hint at so dark a fate.

We should *tak tent*, it suggests,
that he was a *kenspeckle* figure,
much less of a sceptic than Hume,
and not mercantile like Smith.

His use of Scots was unique,
so robust that it inspired Burns,
and preserved how Old Town folk,
citizens of *Auld Reekie*, spoke.

And yet also classically formal,
he was also like a Georgian Horace,
observing the idiosyncracies
of townspeople at work and play.

A true makar, he crafted bright jewels
like *Hallow Fair, The Daft Days,*
On Seeing a Butterfly on the Street,
and *Ode to the Gowdspink.*

Autumn Haiku

(to Alan Spence)

Haar on Arthur's Seat
haiku master in Scotland
now our new Makar

(September 2017)

St. Pancras Old Churchyard

Listening to the chirping of a blackbird
in the churchyard of Old St. Pancras,
I thought of Mary Shelley and her mother,
whose fate was to die giving birth to her.

A coffin-shaped sarcophagus commemorates
Mary Wollstonecraft and her husband
William Godwin; their daughter, rumour has it,
slept beside it on summery London nights.

On a breezy spring day, before I could find
her parents' grave, I saw a dismal crowd
of tombstoned and otherwise memorialized
Victorian worthies; I preferred to dwell

on how she must have noted a blackbird
calling out at twilight. The one I heard
rummaged for twigs to build its nest
on the clock-tower of Old St. Pancras.

Reading *Mrs Dalloway*

Why did Virginia Woolf tell us that Clarissa Dalloway
immersed herself in reading not *War and Peace*,
but Baron Marbot's *Memoir*, on Napoleon's retreat
from a snowbound, deserted Moscow in flames?

Arthur Conan Doyle, like Woolf, knew his Marbot,
so he created in *Brigadier Gerard* a flamboyant officer,
fine hero loyal to a fault, always obedient to Napoleon,
and courageous to the point of recklessness.

Woolf's heroine teasing of an old flame as he fiddles
with a pocket-knife, and prone to idly pare his nails,
cannot compare with the Hussar's battle of wits
with the Spanish brigand, 'El Cuchilo', or 'The Knife'.

Unlike the bold brigadier, Clarissa is full of self-doubt,
her thoughts finely sifted by fleeting impressions,
effervescent one moment, disaffected the next,
bored by parties, but then Big Ben suddenly strikes.

Casting a shadow on her plans to be the perfect hostess,
gracious to every guest, looms Septimus, shell-shocked,
and alienated from high society, his equilibrium at stake.
It's a balance Mrs Dalloway also struggles to maintain.

Septimus is like an alter-ego, and her world seems
too much of a delusion, dangerously unstable,
or liable to disappear capriciously like London fog,
so her preference is for history at close quarters,

Marbot's personal story, not Tolstoy's grand epic.
The Brigadier, very much a Boys' Own hero,
yet also something of a chocolate soldier,
could top a wedding-cake. Woolf 's heroine

looks forward dutifully, her party an affirmation
that life must continue; Conan Doyle's Hussar,
for all his bravado, is just a throwback, only fit
for the sunnier world before 1914.

Bagging Past Poets

No poet's dead who is still read,
so really it's far too condescending
when you declare at poetry readings
that your special treat will be to read
a 'dead poet' before your own poems.

Keats's name wasn't 'writ in water'
as he feared: we still read his poems,
'realms of gold' for us to explore.

Why call him merely a dead one,
as if past poets are game to be bagged
like an iridescent pheasant shot?

Hippos

Consider 'The Hippotamus', a poem
by T.S. Eliot, quirky quatrains about
the Church's ponderous resilience,
then take a look at Alasdair Gray's

series of water-colours, a tribute
to the aquatic pachyderm. It looks
like an Old Testament monster,
his Presbyterian retort to Eliot.

But the hippo was best honoured
by P. G. Wodehouse in Spring Fever:
'Picture a hippopotamus whose love
is returned by his female counterpart

for which it has long entertained
feelings deeper and warmer
than those of ordinary friendship.'
That's really grotesque, and funny,

but it illuminates Eliot's devotion
to the Anglican Church behemoth,
theologically more like Augustine
of Hippo than the portly Henry VIII.

Orwell's Jura Days

(to Ian S. Wood)

Orwell liked to be solitary,
like Crusoe marooned in his island.
Leaving his sister and adopted son
at his landlord's cottage in Jura,

nothing gave him more pleasure,
than to do a spot of exploration.
Hoodie crows congregating
on the dry, stony soil he found

more agreeable than the monks
they amusingly resembled.
From the seashore, spotting seals
swimming happily in the distance

appealed to his sense of wonder,
as did an eagle hovering overhead.
He identified with the hardy crofters,
as he'd done with Spanish Republicans,

but they liked him mainly because
he discreetly kept himself to himself
and was regarded as a kindly gent
who interfered with no one.

He simply went by his real name,
Eric Blair, when he talked to them.
The island postie always took time
to have a dram with his grateful host.

His boat capsized off the island once,
but a lobster fisherman rescued his party.
Luck was with him, as he'd also risked
the lives of his nephew on Army leave

and his little adopted son, Ricky.
They'd barely survived the wrath
of Corryvreckan, fiercest of whirlpools,
and it no doubt shook up his imagination.

Orwell wrote *Nineteen Eighty-Four*
secluded to avoid his London celebrity,
but he had 1947 really on his mind,
suspecting every casual visitor

might be Stalin's secret agent, listening
to the wireless obsessively every morning.
It crackled with news of jackboots stamping
on faces in Poland, Palestine, and Greece.

Crime Writer

I saw you once, sitting still,
gloomy and watchful as a raven.

Your face was so impassive,
craggy with age, a mask
perhaps, an integrity of sorts
was what it conveyed:
the iron will of a writer
knowing that there is much
evil in the world, and you couldn't
just accept that.

You had to square
in your own mind why
it should so often be the case
that exploring motives,
and investigating murders,
grips your readers so much,
even though you make it clear
that it's always a grubby,
stomach-churning business.

Crime for you is the default
mode of the very clever, or
the very stupid and inadequate,
while most simply prefer
to steer clear of the cross-fire.

As you sat there watching
the crowds at a Book Festival,
the sun was insufficiently warm
to banish the chill you feel
at the inescapable approach
of existential oblivion.

You waited for the murderer,
who is taking his time now,
but sooner or later, you knew
it was going to be 'time's up'.

VI

Film

'The task I am trying to achieve, above all, is to make you see.'
D.W. Griffith

Bogart Film Clips

The Somme: Dispatch Rider

A Hollywood Tale

Rod Taylor: A Tribute

Women in Directorial Close-Ups

Indiana Jones

Sapphire

Betrayal

Bogart Film Clips

If you watch *The Maltese Falcon,* Sam Spade,
Humphrey Bogart's tough-minded alter ego,
dodges violent confrontations with the seekers
of the falcon statuette, encrusted with jewels
'from claws to beak'. At the end, he *sends down*
Mary Astor, as his devious client, and lover,
also wanting the falcon. She had killed his partner,
whom he didn't like, and whose wife he bedded,
but because of the crime, his ethics demanded
that 'you're supposed to do something about it.'

Bogart as Rick, the café owner in *Casablanca*
declares 'I stick my neck out for nobody',
such cynical egotism being pure camouflage.
He's really a bitter romantic, in love with Ilsa Lund,
his old flame, played by a radiant Ingrid Bergman,
and married to a Resistance fighter on the run.
'We'll always have Paris': a fond memory shared.
Still a tough guy, and mythically heroic, he signals,
courting danger, his café band to play 'La Marseillaise',
before, in self-defence, he shoots the Nazi commandant.

If 'Bogey' had a dark side, the film which suggested it
was *In a Lonely Place.* He takes on the persona
of 'Dixon Steele', Hollywood-hating screenwriter
and reformed alcoholic, with a penchant for trouble.
His uncontrolled temper makes him a murder suspect.
Gloria Grahame as 'Laurel Gray', his neighbour
and aspiring starlet, provides him with a credible alibi,
and a brief affair. Trapped by self-disgust
which he lashes against her, they avoid each other
at the end, lost in the labyrinth of their block of flats.

Bogart triumphed in his oscar-winning role as 'Charlie',
unsophisticated, but straight-talking, the boozy captain
of *The African Queen,* rust-bucket of a river steamboat
in the Congo. His passenger, prim missionary 'Rose',
pours down his entire supply of gin into the river,
but gradually they attract each other, and come up
with a plan to sabotage a German warship on lake patrol,
via a home-made torpedo. It's not the plot that matters,
but how their cantankerous relationship softens. Both single,
his courage, and rough-hewn sensitivity, win her over.

To Have and Have Not, had Bogart, as Harry 'Steve' Morgan,
captain a fishing-boat in Martinique. He is at first reluctant
to help the Free French there: 'You save France, I'm going
to save my boat,' but he relents, 'Maybe 'cos' I like you.
Maybe 'cos I don't like them,' and he needs the money.
Slim, an acid-tongued lounge singer always one step ahead
of him, was played by Lauren Bacall in her first film.
Twice her age, 'Steve' meets his match when she gives him
an impudent little slap, and teaches him how to whistle.
Bacall recalled that he was truly and completely his own man.

The Somme: Dispatch Rider

Shot at the end of July 1916, recording
The Battle of the Somme, with captions,
was a propaganda film. We watch infantrymen
await the whistle to go over the top and attack
the Germans in their trenches — once Howitzers,
looking monstrous, had done their bit blasting
and bombardiering over No Man's Land.

On screen, German dead outnumbered
the British ones. But the toll of war continued
with intimate close-ups: 'two dumb victims,'
horses 'killed in bringing the field batteries up,'
and, later on, a soldier and his faithful dog,
'who died with his master,' lying side by side,
the battlefield image lingering for a while.

Dispatch riders, possibly luckier, whizzed by
beside official personnel and men on the march.
One sped past an officer cradling a fox cub in his arms,
the regimental mascot 'caught in France.' The rider
on a motorcycle possibly reflected that the officer
was one of his 'betters', this war his 'noblesse oblige,'
and back in 'Old Blighty' a fox-hunting sportsman.

A Hollywood Tale

Robert Mitchum, when rehearsing
Angel Face, slapped the director
deliberately hard just to ask him,
'Is that how I should slap her?'

And that is why he slapped
Jean Simmons, the femme fatale,
right across her face, but scripted
or not, she slapped him right back.

Playing the acme of virtue
in her later film, *Guys and Dolls*,
a lightweight musical, she wore
a red Salvation Army uniform.

So, when gambler Brando
boldly stole a kiss from her,
she slapped him firmly,
but in her heart reluctantly.

Rod Taylor: A Tribute

As an actor, he was not like Marlon Brando,
or even Gregory Peck, but he did have
a distinctive presence of his own, so that
his first leading role in *The Time Machine,*
directed by special effects wizard George Pal,
marked him out a manly, reliable figure.
A brilliant scientist and inventor in that film,
he still seemed ordinary, an embodiment
of rugged civility, and like H.G. Wells himself,
self-confident in his optimistic modernity.

Hitchcock cast him as 'Mitch' in *The Birds,*
a smooth San Francisco lawyer. His encounter
with 'Melanie', Tippi Hedren as a socialite,
headstrong and blonde, aroused her resentment
at his superior air, but his solidity was a notch
more reliable than the elegance of a Cary Grant.
He proved his worth in prevailing against crows,
ravens, gulls, etc. perched on electricity poles,
when he drove off protecting the women in his life:
mother, pre-teen sister, and a battered Melanie.

Antonioni's *Zabriskie Point* had Taylor as 'Lee Allen',
real estate tycoon, bland face of capitalism, intent on
a luxury development in the desert, and appearing only
in brief, but pivotal scenes, all business meetings. 'Daria',
his young aide, puzzled him for preferring meditation.
Driving to Zabriskie Point, she had a clinch with 'Mark',
a fugitive student radical, later killed by the police.
She met her boss at his desert home, its wind-chimes
like those of a Buddhist monastery, but he had no idea
she wanted to meditate on its explosion in slow motion.

Perfectly cast in Jack Cardiff's *Dark of the Sun*,
he personified 'Capt. Curry', a tight-lipped 'action-man'
in red beret, hired for leading a mission to rescue
stranded whites caught up in a civil war blazing
in Congo at the time. Additionally, he aimed to seize
uncut diamonds out of the conflict zone, sharing
his mission with the patriotic Congolese, 'Sgt. Ruffalo',
played by ex-football star Jim Brown. His buddy's murder
by a traitor led him to frenzied, knife-wielding revenge,
so he gave himself up, realizing his heart was dark.

Inglourious Basterds, the Aussie actor's final film,
was Quentin Tarantino's counter-factual thriller
set in an alternative Nazi-occupied France; it had
him appear in a cameo role as Winston Churchill.
Two British officers plotted to trap Hitler himself,
and his gang, in a Paris movie premiere, while Churchill,
in bulldog pose the Karsh photograph made famous,
sat impassively watching them, cigar in hand. He growled
'Brief him!' to the senior officer. H. G. Wells loomed
in Taylor's youth, and in old age, Churchill: icons both.

Women in Directorial Close-ups

Harriet Andersson in *Summer with Monica*,
Bergman's film, plays a teen-age mother at a café.
Her young husband is away at work, and little girl
left with an auntie; after selecting jaunty jazz music
for playing in a juke-box, she lets her furtive lover
light up her cigarette, then stares straight at us,
contempt in her face: *Judge me if you dare!*

Sam Fuller's *Pickup on South Street*,
had Thelma Ritter, playing a wise-cracking,
hardscrabble woman worn down by life;
as she puts it, 'I am an old clock running down'.
Her face in anguished close-up, she faces a killer
wanting information in this Cold War spy thriller.
Defiant to the last, she submits to getting shot.

Alfred Hitchcock's close-up of Grace Kelly
in *Dial M for Murder* has her listening
to her trial for the murder of an intruder
actually sent by her husband to kill *her*. Lights
flash back and forth in lurid technicolor
and illuminate her look of fear as the judge
dons a black cap, and passes sentence.

Gaby Rodgers, a *gamine* with short, blonde hair,
but *not* a star actress, proved to be just right
playing 'Lilly', *femme fatale* in *Kiss Me Deadly*,
Robert Aldrich's take on fifties private investigator
Mike Hammer, played with ruthless bravado
by Ralph Meeker. Gaby's close-up — 'Kiss me, Mike' —
turns into a faint smirk when she shoots him.

Janet Leigh's suspenseful close-up driving her car,
its windshield-wipers fending off the heavy rain,
shows us a trusted office secretary in *Psycho* fleeing
from her theft of money. While discordant music
envelops the soundtrack, she imagines in voice-over
the commotion back at the office, and reveals a hint
of a smile before she stops at the Bates Motel.

Liv Ullmann as a stage actress stricken with silence
and Bibi Andersson as her talkative nurse-therapist,
appeared in Bergman's *Persona*, declared by one critic
as *absurdly important,* meaning it as a compliment.
It has the two women, the silent 'Vogler' and 'Alma',
her guardian, identify so much with each other
in their isolation that their faces merge in close-up.

All these thrawn women found themselves
in tricky situations, trapped in one way
or another by their own actions. David Lynch
in *Dune* was more prophetic: Virginia Madsen,
a free-spirited princess in widescreen close-up,
deep space and shining stars behind her, tells us
of a resources-rich, devastated planet like our own.

Indiana Jones

Your quest was to find the Raiders of the Lost Ark,
Nazi fanatics, searching for them in the souks
and alleyways of a dusty Tunisian town, its crowds
of Arabs looking for bargains, or eager to give you
a sales pitch. You'd already bought a pet monkey
holding on to your shoulder, screeching at anyone
so bold as to get too near his master in a white hat.

While you shield the sun from your eyes, a tall,
bearded, black-robed man rushes out of nowhere
and waves his scimitar at you, his taunting snarl
a real threat. You just shrug your shoulders,
smiling ironically, suave in your self-regard,
and take out a revolver always well-hidden,
but ready to use at any time, like right now.

One shot is all it takes, and your attacker crumbles
before you, his life snuffed out, but not his dreams
of burning skyscrapers. All the others scatter quickly,
or stand in sullen silence. You said about the Nazis
you're hunting: 'I hate those guys!' If these killers
play dirty, *might is right* their creed, take a look
in the mirror: hand on heart, how different are you?

Sapphire

For Sapphire, a drama student, it was the sunset of her life
because she was too secretive.

A rapid-fire, tabloid voice, resembling the voice-over
from Movietone News, emphasized how glamorous
and so very popular she was, dancing wildly in her habitat,
a dimly-lit London night-club, the dancers racially mixed.
That was the trailer.

The film was more nuanced: Police detectives found her,
lying on Hampstead Heath, like a discarded doll,
serenely lifeless as she lay on a desolate patch of grass.

A hint of bleak sunlight seemed all too appropriate,
given it was a murder-scene, and also the morning after
she had danced the night away in grittily garish colour.

Like many fifties crime films, it was routinely moralistic,
and realistically procedural.

The police detectives, one liberal, the other racist,
intrude into the night-club, contemptuous of the revelry,
while questioning everyone, the men wanting to disappear.

I never forgot *Sapphire*, stark prejudice at its heart,
with the murderer, ostensibly respectable, spurred
by resentment at her brother's spirited girfriend
pregnant with a child unlikely to be white.

It ends with one detective, the senior one, arresting
the young woman and telling his partner: 'We didn't
solve anything, we just picked up the pieces.'

I saw it at my local cinema, liking its dark suspense,
but not its insidious message: *Keep to your own kind.*

Betrayal

It was so long ago, the summer of 1962,
I saw *Lawrence of Arabia* with my husband,
an almost guilty pleasure for both of us.

We were well-published historians,
literary critics also, and recently married,
just returned from a university in East Africa
teaching the glories of Romantic poetry
by Shelley, Keats and Byron, not excluding
Burns, since we were proudly Scottish.
His poems, especially *Tam o' Shanter*,
appealed to African students, Border Ballads
in their stark violence even more so.

Africans were optimistic then about
gaining independence from us,
the British colonials, and welcomed
Macmillan's *winds of change* speech.
But they still remembered a rebellion
brutally suppressed. Yet here we were
at a plush cinema in central London,
air-conditioned against a stifling heat-wave:
on screen was a swaggering, blue-eyed,
golden-haired Peter O'Toole riding a camel,
and leading Arabs to revolt, blowing-up
strategic trains against the Turks,
their pashas, in the hot Arabian desert.
Heartbreakingly, his Bedouin friends,
while still wearing their robes in Versailles,
ended up betrayed by his own superiors,
not only the military, but also politicians.

We were so much in love, and at the time
could only thrill at how magnificently heroic
he was; even his tragic end seemed glamorous,
as he swerved to death by motorcycle crash,
his goggles hanging from a branch
which filled up the screen. But neither
of us could foresee, happily expecting
our child as I was, our own break-up.

Later on, I could imagine my husband
preferring to be not like Peter O'Toole,
such an ambiguous hero in his white robes,
but more like the dark-suited Sean Connery,
handsomely ruthless as Bond, James Bond.

VII

History

'The past is never dead. It's not even past.'
William Faulkner

Taigs

Caligula Cornered

Margaret Clitherow

Stalin's Boots

'Conviction Politicians': A Riff on Yeats

1954: A Sleepy Year

Pope Francis

Hamish Henderson's Wartime Interrogations

Taigs

'Why are you so down on,
and find so funny, I asked,
what you call Taigs, the butt
of my friend's sly humour.

'You mean you've lived
all these years in Scotland,
and you don't know
what we mean by Taigs?'

He really disconcerted me,
to his 'Same again?,
I should have replied,
'So what, I don't live

in the same country
as you do, and actually,
in the early days, I like
to think, of a better nation.'

Too timid, I didn't.

Caligula Cornered

Looking at him, I split my sides,
so the senator responded in kind:
'Lord, permit me to share your joke
and honour your sense of humour.

Let these fools who fear you
so needlessly, and so very blind
to your magnanimity, discover
your benevolent humanity':

As he said this, the senator's
right hand gripped too tightly
on his sword, insolent no doubt:
I had to put him in his place.

'Why sure', I said, 'it's your neck
on the line, oh yes, very funny.
Let me tell you, my guard here
could chop it off in a split second!'

But when the guard came
his face was just a shadow
like a lunar eclipse, so dark,
then I knew much too late
that the joke was on me.

Margaret Clitherow

(canonized by Pope Paul VI in 1970)

Consider the prayer-card before me,
it shows an attractive, pensive face,
that of a young woman, her dark hair
enveloped in a bonnet, neck in frilly
ruff and her shoulders covered
by a plain female doublet, an angel
in each corner decorating
her oval portrait, from an engraving
for devotees to contemplate.

She could almost be the Queen
of Spades, since her destiny
was cruelly horrific: pressed
to death, with her spine slowly
broken for refusing to plead
either guilt or innocence,
declaring that 'Having made
no offence, I need no trial'.

She was protecting servants
and her children from testifying
against her, but she was found
guilty of refusing to admit
her role in hiding and assisting
outlaw priests in a secret room
at her house in The Shambles.
She lived there as a respectable,
middle-class woman, her husband,
a devoted, solicitous Protestant.

Her execution on Good Friday
was ordered by officials in York
so reluctant to carry out their task
that they hired town beggars
in their grim and grimy rags
(rather than the town executioner
in full masked paraphernalia)
to fasten her to the fatal rock.

Her martyrdom was so pointless
even in that harsh, sectarian age
that the Virgin Queen, no Queen
of Hearts herself, in this instance
condemned her own judges,
declaring that she *was horrified*
at the treatment of a fellow woman.

Stalin's Boots

Tolstoy in his twilight years,
when his marriage fell apart,
desperately desired a simple life,
so instead of sticking to his last,
that of a celebrity novelist,
and heretical philosopher,
he tried to be a cobbler, just like,
had he known of his existence,
Besarion Jughasvili, skilled
cobbler in provincial Georgia.

Beso, as he was nicknamed,
descended into vagrancy
and alcoholic stupor which
eventually killed him, but
he routinely mistreated *Soso*
his son, who grew up to be Stalin,
whom people called in hushed,
reverent tones, *Our Red Tsar.*

Like Tolstoy, Stalin also lauded
the simple life, and he wanted
it for all his people, provided
they worked overtime all the time,
like the record-breaking Stakhanov,
and not like airy, self-indulgent, and
utopian pipe-dreamers, traitors,
cosmopolitan dilettantes, elitists
and intellectuals like Trotsky.

Stern, yet also avuncular
to his American and British
allies, who regarded him
as their own 'Uncle Joe', he
was determined to avoid
a lazily ineffectual existence
like his loser of a father,
but to be a harsh and unbending
patriarch to all the Russians.

He liked nothing better
than wearing boots
of the finest leather,
and on most days a simple
white tunic, ironically
not unlike pacifist Tolstoy's,
so long as absolutely no one
could be allowed to be free
from their deepest fears,
and that the 'model Russian'
should always 'speak Bolshevik',
exactly as the Party dictates.

He made sure that at any moment
class saboteurs, whether Tolstoy,
or any other traitor, was their hero
or not, would suffer a heart-attack,
or be 'shot on the spot', to realize,
as the song has it, that *these boots
are made for walking, walking
all over you.*

Conviction Politicians: A Riff on Yeats

Dictators like Stalin and Hitler,
despite Yeats, did not 'lack all conviction',
but they were 'full of passionate intensity',
as he stated. These autocrats, cruel
and remorseless, decreed all dissidents
merit only the harshest penalties.

It was a sombre Yeats who warned us
that such absolutists were on the rise,
but he thought mainly about Ireland,
and its eventual descent into Civil War,
due to the purity of national feeling,
and rejection of all compromise.

'No surrender!' was the catchphrase:
North and South, it didn't matter.
James Joyce's disgust was so intense,
he chose 'silence, exile and cunning',
but are we on the same path now,
as monsters maraud the earth again?

Why, then, on pain of being branded
unpatriotic, and elitist enemies
of the people, are we always urged
to adulate conviction politicians?

1954: A Sleepy Year

Churchill was still Prime Minister,
albeit too old the second time around,
the French gave up on remote Indochina,
and Khruschev exulted in the Kremlin,
having triumphed over Stalin's acolytes.
Meanwhile Pope Pius XII decreed 1954
to be a Marian Year, in sacred honour
of the Blessed Virgin. A shrine to Mary,
not exactly well-kept, is still there,
and largely forgotten by passing students,
in the side-lawn of the former War Hospital,
Craiglockhart, now Napier University, famous
for Owen's and Sassoon's wartime friendship.
Neither had much faith in any Divinity.

UFOs dominated the front pages regularly,
now yellowed in the archives, of the tabloids
but one at least, classified 'Top Secret',
was just an experimental prototype
of the Harrier Jump Jet, flown by a test pilot,
in Nottinghamshire, its apparent tentacles
and antennae straight out of *The War
of the Worlds*. But to Roman Catholics,
less credulous about alien space invaders,
UFOs were just a hallucinatory superstition;
they scorned belief in 'close encounters
of the third kind', whether friendly or not.
A papal dogma they accepted and revered,
instead, was Mary's Immaculate Conception.

Pope Francis

(after Giuseppe Belli, Romanesco poet)

What can I say? That's what I like, my friend:
each to his taste, yet consider him for a while.
This Pope, popular with the media, has a smile
for everybody, is likeable and unpretentious.

For all that, if he doesn't change his views,
it would be preferable, I must insist,
for Pope Francis to be like retired Benedict,
who banned 'Liberation Theology' as vile.

What kind of pope is this, who gives offence
to bishops protecting unfairly accused priests,
who even questions belief in hell, is he dense?

To top it all, his pastoral care is so bland,
he sidestepped the abortion referendum.
How humiliating for the Church in Ireland!

Hamish Henderson's Wartime Interrogations

A glassy stare from the brutish face
of blue-eyed SS Colonel Herbert Kappler,
with his *Schmisse* scar prominent,
trying to outstare me. How pathetic!

The man before me looked disdainful,
he lacked all honour. As reprisal
for a Partisan ambush in Rome,
he ordered 335 hostages murdered:

men and women of all ages, classes,
and walks of life, in the Ardeatine Caves.
To stir his conscience, if he had one,
I read to him an Italian *Lament* poem,

Corrado Govoni's elegy for Aladino,
his son shot dead. But it was no use,
he only made my blood run cold
with his hypocritical response:

An old father's grief is for me
something sacred. More routinely,
I interrogated a Lance Corporal
in the Afrika Korps, defeated,

but an enemy whose honour
did not depend on a duelling scar.
He resisted every query by stating
only name, rank and serial number.

He really was an awful pain,
but I don't think he was a Nazi,
not a true-believer, just human,
all too human.

Epilogue

'Poetry's of no interest if it's written by oneself, It's only of interest if it comes from beyond.'
Seamus Heaney

Owl at Twilight

Owl at Twilight

'The owl of Minerva spreads
its wings only at dusk' Hegel insisted
in his oracular mode. His riddle
meant to explain the wisdom
of hindsight as the key to history.
But for the owl, as it looks for prey,
determined to reclaim the night,
the past means nothing at all:

It can see more clearly in the dark;
daylight, after all, only makes it drowsy,
hence the owl alights on the nearest branch,
ready by instinct when the sun rises,
to welcome sleep, and renew itself,
once more to spread its wings at dusk.

Lightning Source UK Ltd.
Milton Keynes UK
UKHW021012111021
392014UK00009B/166